life THROUGH
poetry

Happy Birthday, and

Enjoy!
from Ron & Tish

Carol Sheldon

life THROUGH

poetry

written by
Paul A. Sheldon

TATE PUBLISHING & *Enterprises*

Published by Tate Publishing & Enterprises, LLC
127 E. Trade Center Terrace | Mustang, Oklahoma 73064 USA
1.888.361.9473 | www.tatepublishing.com

Tate Publishing is committed to excellence in the publishing industry. The company reflects the philosophy established by the founders, based on Psalm 68:11,
"The Lord gave the word and great was the company of those who published it."

Book design copyright © 2008 by Tate Publishing, LLC. All rights reserved.
Cover design by Lindsay B. Behrens
Interior design by Isaiah R. McKee

Published in the United States of America

ISBN: 978-1-60462-740-4
1. General Interest: Literature & the Arts: Poetry   2. Poetry: General

08.03.10

Dedication

I dedicate this book to three very spe-
cial ladies in my life.
First I would like to thank my wife for her
help and support. She has been an encour-
agement to me from the very start.

Ginny was a great surprise in our lives as you will
see in one of the poems within this book. It was a
beautiful experience to see them both together for
the first time after so many years. The happiness
I saw in their faces was tremendous, and became
the inspiration in writing many of my poems.

Last, but far from least is my niece, Victoria"
Tori" Peddicord, for her help putting this
book together. Without her expertise the
book might never have been published.

This book is my way of saying thank you
to each one of them in a special way.
God bless them all!

Poetry

It's what I see to be true.

The idea of poetry is to talk with your heart.
There are people who may think it not very smart.
Getting my thoughts out for others to understand,
At least for me it is poetry to command.
No matter what you might think. Poetry works for
my sanity's sake.
The inner voice we've written down is never a fake.
When words come from within,
it's straight from the heart.
This voice written on paper I feel is truly smart.
It is the soul that makes this a loving art.

Author's Comment:

*It's my opinion, but I feel that poetry is
short because it's a thought that creates emo-
tion in the poet just wanting to get out.*

The Author growing up in Country Life

Age 8

Age 15

Age 15

Age 19

Growing AND Learning

My Country

This is for those who love plenty of space for good living.

The farms are left empty, back
to nature they did give.
The people went to the city for
good jobs they did find.
This is going on in the hills of the state where I live.
Now in the winter the
country is cold, dark, and gray.
Well I guess most of the time
in the house I will stay.
Listen to the lonesome cry of the
coyote calling for his mate.
All of nature comes knocking on my gate.
Look out the kitchen window at those
bucks searching for their doe.
Such artistry here in the woodland just goes to show
The perfect love that God wants us to know. I'd like
to invite you to see this place I have come to love so!

Author's Comment:
Most people think that New York State is like New York City, but it's not. I feel it is truly a beautiful state.

A Day At The Farm

*If you work around animals, you know what I'm
talking about.*

Cows are in the barnyard,
the chickens in the pen.
The dog is up and standing guard.
Think all is going better than it's ever been.
Well, coming 'round the corner is the family cat.
She got the dog in a complete uproar,
scared the horse, and he kicked down the barn door.
The cows got out, and ran away.
Look, they are over at the
neighbors' munching on his hay.
The neighbor called using a
foreign language because he's mad.
The kids can't find their cat, so they are sad.
All this because that old house cat has been bad.

Pluckin' Chickens

*This poem goes out to those old farm
boys from the 40s and 50s.*

Pluckin' chickens is no job for me.
"Please don't make me!" is my plea!
Got to pop its head off, and let fall to
the ground.
A big pot of boiling water it's got to be.
Yah, take the chicken by the legs, and dunk.
Then grab those feathers by the hunk.
Pulling them off is easy, don't you see?
The only problem is those darn old feathers
get all over me.
They stick all over right where they land.
Plucking chickens I just can't stand!

Author's Comment:
*Back when I was a kid, one of my jobs was to get the
chicken cleaned for Sunday dinner. It was not the best job
in the world.*

Another School Year

I thought I'd try being a kid again, and see how it would be.

Oh, Mom, do I have to get up?
I really feel sick today.
I have nothing to wear, I say.
Breakfast, huh? No way!
Look, Mom, I've done my homework.
Don't you think Eddy is a jerk?
I listen closely when the teacher speaks.
Judy wears too much make-up on her cheeks.
I don't quite understand math fully.
Mike, he's a dead-beat, and a bully.
In gym we are playing basketball.
I hate it when boys fool around in the halls.
The history teacher gave us lots of
homework, and that's a bummer.
A month left, and I'm already thinking of summer!

Back Then

This is for the tender hearts in the last days.

As I look at the ways of today, and I
see the morals of the devil.
People want to have more freedom, they say.
To do just what they want, and have their own way.
The code of ethics exists, but not as it should.
In these times the world calls evil good.

Looking back to the times past when
people were afraid to fly,
it didn't seem possible that they
would soon flock to the sky.
Remember back when you needed something done.
There was always someone ready to serve.
Now you ask, and they look at you
like, "You sure have nerve".

When a man went wrong he was held to blame.
Today it's his environment in which he came.
People looked at our flag as sacred, its
beauty showing a country free.
All our citizens proud to see it unfurled.

It is true freedom that could be
seen all over the world.

In all the conflicts, and war which we never choose,
There was never a thought that we might loose.
Now we are in fear at our border,
as we sit here in a war-torn corridor.

It is time, I say, to get back to "In God We Trust"!
This is truly a must, before our
country is turned to a pile of dust.

A Change Of Life

This is to all who need a reason to change.

The harder you work, the deeper in debt.
You draw a larger gross, but just look what you net.
Despair and sorrow are the cards you were dealt.
You wanted to know, well, that's how yesterday felt.
Wishing all was changed so it would be right.
Time has come in life to look
back to that painful sight.
Seeing the wrongs that have been done,
you want to quit everything, and run.

Now, I've got a friend in whom I can count.
"His praise," I am so happy I will shout.
My days are true blessings without a doubt.
Life is worth the living,
something I gladly talk about.
You wanted to know; well, this is
what makes life so good to me.
Jesus is my Savior, and it's him I'm happy to see!!

Author's Comment:
*I wish and pray that all could have what I have with my
Lord Jesus Christ!*

Teen Feelings

To all my teen friends, I wish you well!

Although you may think what I say is very odd.
Mother gave me life, with the help of God.
Oh, I didn't forget that Father put in his help too.
As parents you are the best, but like others, realize
owners you can not do.
Please understand we are put
on this earth to be free.
I know you care so much, you have dreams of what
I'll grow up to be.
Let me go, and guide me with what you know.
I'll make you proud of what has become of me.
All your love and guidance will
make me strong enough.
To be what I want to be.

Teach Them Well

To all the loving parents of the world, God bless.

God bless the little children of the world.
Little girls with their pretty hair in curls.
Little boys full of mischief, and joy.
They don't even play with the same kinds of toys.
Teach them right by respecting others' wishes.
Both boys and girls should learn to wash dishes.
Children should do chores to promote humility.
Moms and Dads work together to show stability.
Little boys will grow up to be men of conviction.
Little girls will grow up to know no restriction.
Give a child a chance to know the truth, and they
will help change other youth.
I'm wishing their future all the very best.
God in their lives, they'll be truly blessed.

Author's Comment:
*I love children, but it is the parents that make a good
person out of that little child!*

Growing Up

A little love goes a long way!

One heart, one love, and one rose.
Each little child is a treasure that grows.
Searching for the reason for it all?
Learning to pick yourself up each time you fall.
Feel the love of God, in the soul of Mom and Dad.
Being born to this life I feel both lucky and glad.
I'm looking at the children all around the world.
Too many have no life, no love, and no one to care.
Their lives are filled with darkness, and despair.
If only we could give what we
have for others to share.
Then all little children would have a life to start.
It can be done with preparation of your heart!

Mother's Little Baby

To all young mothers everywhere.

Love that swells within our land.
The tender touch of a mother's hand.
Look at the beauty of spring, and all
growing things.
Grass, flowers, and birds that sing.
Warm breezes blow, and cool waters flow.
The mother's love which little baby knows.
The safety within it's mother's reach.
Lessons of life to her baby she'll teach.
In babies bed as soft as a puffy white cloud.
Mommy and Daddy are truly very proud!

Author's Comment:
*That is where love really starts, with God's Gift to the
loving parents!*

Teddy Bear Sleeps

This is about children with cancer.

Hi, my name is Amanda.
My little teddy bear is a panda.
I can't go out today, it's too windy.
My best friend in school is Cindy.
Mommy told me yesterday what the doctor said.
Today I'm stuck here with teddy in bed.
Mommy said that I'm very sick with
something called cancer.
She was crying as she told me to be
brave because she has no answer.
My friend comes to visit me, and
it makes me very glad.
I hate what I have, because it makes
Mommy and Daddy so sad.
Everyone says I'm very brave to
live with what I've got.
What they don't understand is I'm really not.
All those tomorrows that I cannot see,
God will come soon 'cause it is meant to be.

Child Without Life

To married couples with children looking to divorce,
don't!

Why don't Mommy and Daddy love me anymore?
I try real hard to make it like it was before.
Daddy is gone, and Mommy works all the time.
We can't afford much, and I don't even have a dime.
I do things, I know not why.
I feel my world is gone, and I want to die.
I haven't seen my daddy since, I can't remember.
There is no more Christmas in December.
No one cares anymore, so I'll run away.
I have a lot on my mind, but nothing to say.
Mommy and Daddy, I'll be good if
only you'll make things all right.
I need you both to love me, and hug me real tight!

Author's Comment:
It makes me sick to see children passed around from pillar
to post. Don't get me wrong, there are exceptions.

Life From My Eyes

To life and the beauty of it!!!

The blue of sky,
the green of trees,
That's what gives life to me.
The smell of flowers,
the warmth of sun,
love of life is full and fun.
As we grow, and learn to feel, we
find that love is truly real.
Years go by, and folks turn gray.
Take pride in life as life is today.
Time is come when life is through.
Now I pass this love on to you.
A land full of corruption that
keeps us from being free.
Chemical air, how bad it stinks.
Polluted water, it's not fit to drink.
Greed and crime, this seems to be our song.
The caring people, are they almost gone?
This, my son, is all I may have to pass on.
Oh, why don't we wake up to
see what we have done?

Look around, what you see doesn't have to be.
When we walk together with God, all
that can be changed, don't you see?
Truth, happiness, and freedom will be
the gift God gives you and me.
It is then I'll feel special, new, and proud
to pass God's work on to you.

Country Life

To the 1950s!

Smell Mama's cookin' in the kitchen.
Papa, the horse to the wagon needs hitchin.'
No time for a whole lot of playin.'
Got to get busy on the hayin.'
Listen to that song of the meadow lark.
It gets very quiet just after dark.
A melodious sounds of frogs a croakin.'
Can't go to town, because the wheel
on the wagon is broken.
I just can't wait till fall.
The leaves on the trees are changin' color, that's all.
Winter is coming up so we got corn to shuck.
Mama has gone to town to get her hair curled.
I wouldn't change this life for the world!

Author's Comment:
Yes, poor folks still had horses back then!

Life on the farm in my teenage years wasn't all work.

Lots of good times and good memories.

Halloween

This is for all my friends that celebrate Halloween.

Halloween is in a dismal time of year.
It is the changing of the seasons when the
darkness comes near.
Time for strange noises coming from that old
house across the street.
Wait till dusk to take the
little ones out to trick or treat.
Stop at that old house, there's an ugly old witch
I want you to meet.
She is stirring a pot of bad-smelling brew.
The drink she will be glad to give to you.
Listen and hear the howls, screams, and a dead
pirate's cry.
The ghosts and goblins are all around, just
to bring on your fears.
Yes, October is that time of year!

Author's Comment:
It is a time for a great imagination.

Harvest Feast

*To my friends that don't celebrate Halloween
because of their faith in God.*

Harvest Feast is at the time of year when all
the crops are in.
We come together to celebrate the bountiful life
we are livin.
Just settle back to reflect on all the wonder that
God has given.
A great day of fellowship I have decided.
Praising God for all He has provided.
We'll sing some songs, and talk over old times.
Mothers are telling their
children little nursery rhymes.
All the people at our church gather together.
Looking to the time when we'll be with our
Savior, forever.

Chuck

This is to my brother Charles on his
60th birthday, 28 October 2001.

Try hard to look into your heart.
I want to write this poem without upsetting
your apple cart.
So start out with a beat of the drum.
Thinking back to the child I came from.
Looking into the future is harder then it seems.
Out of school, and to the door of life.
Time of searching for that special person,
Melanie, my wife.
God in my life makes the when, where, and why.
Truth and love make for a strong family to be.
One beautiful girl came along to make us three.
Little Denise is true happiness for you and me.
Along came a handsome fellow just a few years later.
Charles, Jr., make this life's road a little bit greater.
Thank God for a
wonderful wife to share this life with.
Then came Jessica, another lovely
gift that God did give.
Sometimes I feel humble looking at the life
God gave me to live.

True blessings and another birthday
here at home, safe and sound,
with loved ones all around.

Author's Comment:
*I wrote this to sound as if Charles was thinking of the
wonders that happened in his life. His nickname is
"Chuck."*

my brother Charles, and his family

Life!

This is for my Uncle on my wife's side of the family.

Growing up from Abraham's seed,
I love being a kid, yes indeed.
Family love carries me through.
That's one debt that never comes due.
A young man bright-eyed and full of hope,
I looked for the life's work in which I could cope.
I decided to work for the railroad line.
Trains coming and going everywhere,
I loved working at the roundhouse there.
For a long time I gave my blood, sweat, and tears.

So now comes the retirement years
Things change so fast it leaves my mind in a whirl.
Thank God for my love, a special girl.
Together we walk hand in hand to our twilight time.
You know, I'm looking forward to heaven,
so I don't have to grow old in a second life!

Author's Comment:
*My Uncle Bill was in the hospital very sick at the age of
ninety years old. We wanted something for him to think
about because he was giving up, so I wrote this.*

The Man (as I saw him)

This poem was written for my step-
father as I sat at his deathbed.

He was a hardened man as I saw him at first.
A man not at all well versed.
A man of extreme rough exterior,
A man I felt at first as quite inferior.
I know I took him wrong back when, because
I took no time to know him then.
I didn't see the love and kindness he seemed to hide.
When I did, his strengths came shining
through as though a great tide.
His power was not for man to boast, for I felt
it came from the Holy Ghost.
A heart of gold, and love not denied.
I found a friend I'll shout with pride!

Author's Comment:
I felt sorrow as most people do, but I also felt happy
and proud to have known him. Because of him, my life
has been truly blessed!

A Psalm To You,
Dear Friend

This poem was written for my stepfather at his funeral.

Your first day with God I know is
filled with joys unknown.
Your life fulfilled, and all the pain left behind.
Loved ones miss you as ten-
der thoughts are on their minds.
When time is done, and God brings us too, what
a reunion with others along with you.
The world has taught us to feel sadness and sorrow,
but that I do not know.
What was hard for me to say at times, my heart and
pen can say. You'll never be forgotten.
Love from me to you, my dear friend, sends
this note your due!

Author's Comment:
*I read both this and "The Man" for his friends and
relatives there for him at the end.*

Gerty

This is for the wonderful ladies at the
Chenango Valley Home.

Gerty is a friend in memory now.
Our love goes to dog heaven somehow.
We've gotten so much of her trust.
She didn't make the return a must.
Looking to a friend that really cared,
Show her all the love you truly dare.
Gerty is the friend in memory now.
I pray I'll see her when I get to heaven,
somehow.

Author's Comment:
It is a wonderful thing to see when a pet can bring so
much happiness to the elderly stuck in nursing homes.

Tasha

"The family dogs and what they mean to us!"

As I look down from my heavenly home,
I'll be with you in memory so you'll never be alone.
Looking back to the day of my birth,
you gave me the feeling of value and worth.
I was born on a fine day in May 1991,
the beautiful daughter and not a son.
I was healthy, and happy learning to play and run.
I had a good reason because my
new name was Johnson.
I found my job in life was to care
for a boy named Mike.
I grew to love him, even in his teenage strife.
He grew into a strong and handsome man.
Then fell in love, and marriage he did plan.
He took me into a new world I tried to understand.
Time went by, and soon he brought me a new
human puppy.
She is a beautiful baby girl, not a guppy.
Allison is the little one's name.
We would run and play a wonderful game.
I knew the job, like with Mike, was the same.

We'd visit Grandma for great
meals and a special treat.
This was a dog's life, but it can't be beat.
My puppy, "Sissie," and I had many a good time.
The pain of getting old was start-
ing to make me whine.
God told me that my job here was done.
Now I wait in heaven for you so we can again run.

Author's Comment:
*This was written as a tribute to Mike and Allison
for showing Tasha so much of their love.*

The beautiful work from the caring hands of my loving wife. This was made for our nephew. I was truly blessed when I met this wonderful lady.

Hands Of Love

This is a special blanket just for you.

As you look at it, it will show you love,
that is true.
Love is what will last through all the year.
Love from those that you hold so dear.
Friends that you have met in the past,
are wonderful memories that will last.
This special blanket is full of loving hands. You can
keep this memory no matter what life commands.
Hands that have held you tenderly near.
Hands that have pointed the way and made
life very clear.
This special blanket is full of names
of the people that care.
Names of loved ones, your life they did share.
As you go on through a new part of your life, add
on names, including your wife.
Don't let it stop till the very end.
It is the memory of all who are friends!

Author's Comment:
*This I wrote to our nephew Ben after I looked at the
blanket my wife made for him.*

This is my wife Violet.

My Love

To my wonderful wife!

Long ago when I was young, I found
a woman, loving and shy.
I longed to know her, but knew not why.
After a few times together I knew she was the one.
A true and deep love here under the sun.
I had to leave, and go away, even though
I wanted very much to stay.
Through letters that we noted, I
was becoming quite devoted.
Today, looking back over all those years,
we conquered our problems, strife, and fears.
Feelings of love in every word we talk.
As time goes by, we don't look at the clock.
A love like ours is as strong as a rock.

Author's Comment:
*I really don't know how she has put up with me
this long!*

My Wife

*To my wife for so many years of being
my comfort and strength!*

The things of wonder and memories I gain.
She is to me the wind and the rain.
The happiness, sorrow, and pain,
all the truths that run through my brain.
This is the lady, my lady, and my life.
This lady to warm my heart is truly my wife.

My memories as I'm looking into the past.
The world around us is to make up the cast.
The present to live that sets the stage.
The wonders of life are in this crazy age.
Courage to look ahead to our future as time flies by.
Closely we walk towards the heavenly sky.
This lady to warm my heart is truly my wife.

Author's Comment:
*My wife and I have had thirty outstanding years together.
Now that is true love!*

In My Heart, For My Sister

A long, long time has gone by
With neither a hello, or good bye
Always thinking of the how come or why.
The years just keep creeping slowly by.
The love we once knew has all but gone, I fear.
A life without her has simply brought me to tears.
A computer I bought to keep me occupied.
Search for my roots, I decide.
This generation is such a wonderful age.
The computer put into motion, and set the stage.
With just a click, click of the switch,
Wow, my sister was found!
Well, a hurry-scurry getting ready, and
away we did go, vacation-bound.
We met, hugged, talked, and cried a little.
It's funny how life can be such a riddle.
The love we had has come back
after thirty long years.
Now that happiness has chased
out all those lonely tears.
I thank God for my sister, and can't
wait each time another
visit is near!

Author's Comment:

I wrote this poem for my wife. She has just found her sister after around thirty years. This reunion was a godsend that has made her extremely happy.

In The Wind Of Time

When two hearts meet, and those
wedding bells do chime,
what was yours and mine has
come to be ours in time.
The wind of life blows warm and sweet
as our lives are entwined.
Truth and love are ours to cherish and to keep.
All the treasures of life together you and I will reap.
God's blessing will come each day to us.
Guidance, wisdom, and a message we can trust.
God as our foundation, the life we have together
for eternity we'll keep.

God, protect us when life's stormy winds blow.
When our two hearts grow as through life we go.
Lord, help us to keep all our priorities in a row.
Let us stand on Thy foundation as
the seed of life we do sow.
Looking back to when two hearts met, and
those wedding bells did chime.

When the time is come, and we are old,
the wind of time has become just a small breeze.

We will walk hand in hand together, you and me.
Just remember back to when the wind of life
blew warm and sweet.
When two hearts have met, and
those wedding bells did chime,
all those happy years will seem
just a short way in time.

Author's Comment:
*Stand fast, and look at the whole picture. The good times,
and the bad times, but do it together with God!*

Life Long Friends

*To all the wonderful people I've
met in my life, God bless!*

Friendship has always been a for-
tune in the treasures of my heart.
You have to realize people are
human, and make mistakes
from the start.
A sister or a brother—closer they could never be.
Friends are Friends within me for all eternity.
A person you can tell all your troubles to.
Go and tell others are some-
thing they just wouldn't do.
Loving and caring truths are what you can share.
This is the person I'd give my life for.
True friendship should never end, and
that is for sure!

The Color OF Love

This is a special blanket made just for you.

Let it surround you with the
warmth of love that is true.
In your travels no matter where in the world,
This love goes with you as your life is unfurled.
The beauty in color is a reflection of peace and love,
the security of knowing our Heavenly Father above.
This special blanket is made with lov-
ing hands that truly care.
Just a little something to show there are people your
burdens, you can share.
As you walk through life you are not alone.
Family around you sets a loving tone.
You can look to your future with confidence
in all that you do.
Know in your heart that our prayers will
always be with you!

Author's Comment:
*This I wrote after looking at the blanket my wife made
for our niece. The name of the blanket design is "Trips
around the World."*

Help The Child Grow

This is for all the caring parents.

Day to day living is how they grow.
Learning the way they think life ought to go.
Don't blame the school when the child goes bad.
The way some children are made to live could
make you very sad.
What they see in you and me is more of what
they will end up to be.
Looking around at good and bad, they decide
what they want to see.
From all that is living around them most always
is what they will know.
Only through the time of love and caring that you
invest in them can they master their own destiny.

Author's Comment:
*We know how great a parent is by how good the child
becomes an adult!*

Freddy

*For all the lonely little children that
have no one that cares.*

It was a tiny, little teddy.
Its name just happened to be Freddy.
He lived in a tiny shack at the edge of town.
It was not much to see, because
it was about to fall down.
Nothing to eat, and too cold to sleep,
go outside, but the snow is quite deep.
A man passing by took time to peek.
It made him so sad he could not speak.
The sight of a little boy gone cold,
he was on a tattered old lounge chair, as it was told.
It seems as if no one cared, except Freddy,
his tiny little teddy bear.

Remember Me

To a friend when her husband passed away.

Remember me not in these last days.
Look back at the wonderful life we had with praise.
Thank God for the love we always knew.
How as the years went by, our love grew.
Many a year has passed away, and with
a great woman, I must say.
As I watch over you from heaven above,
remember you are my one, and only, true love!

A Prayer For Eddie

*This is for darlee 77 and fam-
ily. I am honored to be a friend!*

There is a dear lady I have come to know.
The way she tells of your love,
and how she loves you so.
The tension and torment as she
cares for others to her will go.
I pray for her son Eddie, "With
thy healing hands, you give
him his eyes to see.
Oh, and Lord please give Tony a life filled with glee.
Give this wonderful family your
helping hand," is my plea.
"Dear Lord, bless the love of all mothers.
because they spend their life caring for others.
I pray you show the world all of their love.
It's the closest to that from above!"
Amen

Author's Comment:
*Thank you for being a friend!
This is a friend I met online.*

THE Calendar Year

The Calendar

January is the spanking new start
to a wonderful new year.
February is the time of cold nights, so
sit by the fire with a cup of cheer.
March is the month of all kinds of weather—
warm, cold, and maybe bad storms, I fear.
April is a time of renewal in a
beautiful green with plenty of rain.
May is when I have to get ready
for gardening all over again.
June here in the North Country is alive
with hard work on the farm.
July is a time to celebrate our
independence and good old American charm.
August looks to the abundance of love God
has laid on this land without fear of harm.
September all the children are
getting ready for another school year.
October is the time of ghosts,
goblins, and ugly old witches to fear!
November is a time of peace in your heart
and Thanksgiving because God is near.

December is the time of remembering our Savior's
birth, and thoughts of brotherly love are so clear.
Now that we have gone through this time in our life,
Try to reflect on why we are here.
Praise God, and honor Jesus' birth!
Know the truth and what it is worth!

January

Father Time has gone, and Baby New
Year just came through the door.
Here is the "January thaw," then
back to winter once more.
Cold crisp mornings as the temperature will dip.
I'll stay by the fire as a cup of coffee I sip.
Looking out the window at the birds as they feed,
get a good book, and settle down to read.
~OR-~
Bundle up, and go out in the
cold, white winter snow.
At the top of the hill we stand looking below.
Hop on the sled, and away we will go.
Fun, laughter, and singing songs we all know.
Take it easy—January isn't over, and
there are eleven months to go!

February

The groundhog comes out to see
if winter will go away.
Winter is getting old, and I wish it would not stay.
It is time of love, and giving a
valentine or two will be okay.
Washington and Lincoln are
observing their birthdays.
I say, "If spring comes early, it
would be nice anyway."
Well, February is a short month even
though winter is still at bay.
March is on the way, but it could
come faster, I will say.
In fact it would be great if it were already May!

March

This is a month of great history, and all Presidents' Day.

March is the month of winter's last fight.
Winds blow too hard to fly a kite.
Longer is the day, and shorter the night.
Can't guess the weather, try as you might?
It may snow an inch, or a foot.
Sap from the maple tree coming up from the root.
The wonders of spring just coming awake,
it's time to get out your hoe, and your rake.
It's time to plan what you'll put in your garden.
Well, if I'm too early, please beg my pardon.
Looking for more of that warm sunshine,
I'm ready to leave that cold weather behind.
Let's be thankful for what we've got.
Thinking of this month of March quite a lot,
say what we may, but summer it's not!

Author's Comment:
I'm old, and my bones don't like winter!

Ground Hog's Day

Mister groundhog is so chunky and fat.
If it wasn't for your size you'd look like a rat.
Sometimes you're hard at work dig-
ging in the ground.
Then again sunning yourself, "lazy like" on a mound.
Eat all summer, then all winter sleep.
Along about February they say
you come out for a peep.
Is your shadow up, or is your shadow down?
Please don't keep this old winter around!
We really don't want to hear what you have to say.
Contrary to legend, stay in your
hole 'til April or May!

April

As I look out my window this crisp winter's morn,
I feel a bit dismal and forlorn.
Looking just a little closer at the
birds there eating corn.
April is the time of rain, and lots of mud,
and all the trees, and flowers to bud.
The deer are in the meadow
showing who's the biggest stud.
See the beautiful rainbow up above.
Feel the grandeur of nature's love. It's
the time of the last snowflake.
You can bet all of nature is coming awake.
Yes, April is that time when winter finally ends.
So we can get outside, and start the gardening trend.

Author's Comment:
Coming into a new season we tend to get charged up for
the outside work ahead.

May

A memorial of loving people in our past,
and armed forces service duty.
A tribute to our mothers: set aside this day.
Give her the best of rest, and all the love you can,
I would say.
Time to get out and go for a walk,
enjoying the warm sun along the way.
Thanking God for all the wonders He has sent
us this day.
May is truly a beautiful month to picnic and
just let your mind go astray.
Take a little nap as on a grassy lawn you lay.

My Love For Mother's Day

*This was written on the mother's day
just before she passed away.*

Mother, dear Mother, my love for you is strong.
It will last from morning 'til
night, then back to dawn.
From the day of my birth through the day I became
a man, your love and
devotion shaped me for what I am.
Thank you, dear Mother, for
the wonders of my past.
It filled me with love, the kind that will last.
I know I could never repay you for
this road of life I am on.
Straight and true with God, and
you to heaven's land.
The times we've had
walking through life hand in hand.
This at last I want with all my heart to say:
God bless and keep you this very
precious Mother's Day.

June

Let's vacation out on the beach collecting shells.
Maybe go on a walk in the forest taking in all
the wonderful smells.
Watch the farmers take the cows to pasture and
bring in the hay.
Looking around at the beauty
of nature, "Praise God!"
is what I'd say.
Set your mind on what Flag Day is all about.
Freedom to live the way God
meant us to with no doubt.
June is the halfway mark of one great year
we can shout.
Father's Day, and thoughts of
family—isn't that what
life is all about?

Father's Day

I ask, Father where did you go? I wish
of you, Father, I did know.
I never had the chance to feel your love.
Just hoping you are looking down from above.
I wish at times of you I could remember.
Our lives with you from January to December.
No one talks of you—the things
I really want to know.
I feel you must have been a good man
because Mom loved you so.
Time has gone by, and we are all getting old.
The time is coming when my
body will also grow cold.
When I get to heaven, what a day that will be!
All of us together, the family, friends, you, and me!

July

Vacation or maybe just gone fishing is a mode that
we know will not last.
A great life because of the
meaning behind Independence Day.
The special Americans that have gone on, you can
say, "They are the
reason for freedoms that guide our way."
July is an outstanding month to
forget the work and go play.
If it weren't for a few
thunderstorms it would be the best.
A good month for a party, so invite a guest.
July is about over, so get back to
work, and maybe some rest.

The Beauty In Summer

I don't know, but I'd say the category should be love.

Working for a living and making such a fuss.
So many times we're too busy to
see the wonders around us.
Take time to feel the greatness of
nature as it happens to be.
You'll find that the best things in life are free.
The sweet smell of pine, or a soft
breeze under the old apple tree.
The coolness of water flowing
gracefully down from the hill.
Listening to the lonely sound of the
whip-poor-will. Wild flowers up in the woods,
some real bright, and others a bit duller.
Looking down the valley at the explosive color.
As the wind gets stronger, and the tree limbs bend.
The warm sun of summer must come to its end.

August

This is start of harvest, and the
garden is in full array.
Bring in the vegetables to be canned;
until winter they will stay.
Fresh sliced tomatoes, and cucum-
bers we'll have to eat.
Sweet corn in abundance is a family treat.
Everyone in the car, and head to
town the neighbors to meet.
Set up a stand at the farmer's
market selling produce on the street.
We'll have a grand old time
getting news from friends we greet.
Be thankful for a wonderful crop
that God has passed on to us.
Wait for Grandpa to pray or
Grandma will make a fuss.
This is one great time in the month of August!

September

September is a wonderful time of year for all to see.
It's a time for learning, not just for
kids, but also you and me.
Young people headed for
college, and children back to school.
The education we get will help us
tomorrow, so don't be a fool.
Education that we had
yesterday was very good, but now
it's up for renewal.
This is a time of joy and care when
we all meet at the state fair.
We go to have fun, enjoy each
other, and the great smell
in the air.
This is the time when farmers' prize
crops and animals, they share.
September is the time of year when
most people show how much
they really care.
This is the month you city folks
should come visit the country
if you dare.

The Brat

*To those naughty little boys that made it out of
School alive!*

Going to town with Mama to get new clothes for
school this fall.

Start by trying out for football.

No, no, you dummy! Not in study hall.

It's a rough, tough time being in school.

You've got to try your best to follow the rule.

Picking on the girls when I was a kid.

Did I really do that? Yup, I did—I did!

Got caught throwing spit balls in school?

Well, it isn't so bad sitting here on the
dunce stool.

Did I take Annie's pony tail and stick it in
the ink well?

Then made her promise not to tell.

Went and put a snake in the teacher's seat?

Oh, she didn't think it was neat.

She told me if I didn't watch out, the grade
I would repeat.

At our reunion she told me I was a brat in school.

As hard as I tried I couldn't follow the rule.

Picking on all the girls when I was a kid.

Did I do that?

Yup, I did—I did!!

Author's Comment:
Please, this is not me!

October

The changes of the season, wonders in action!
Summer is almost gone, and chill is in the air.
Daylight is short, and darkness replaces it there.
Little faces turn rosy red with a very big grin.
To look back now would be a sin.
Almost always this is when the snow will begin.
October is when we put the summer things away.
We replace them with our winter toys to play.
A time for parties, and lots of good food to eat.
Little ghosts and goblins come out to trick or treat.
Wild varmints ready to
hibernate are digging in deep.
The trees and plants are tired, and going to sleep.
Canadian geese are headed south,
an appointment to keep.
All the harvest is in, and winter is coming on strong.
I think I'll get a good book, and sit by the fire
where I belong.
Just maybe invite the neighbor in for hot chocolate,
and sing old time songs.
That is the way October is supposed to go.
People, a warm fire, and songs we all know.

Author's Comment:

*All the hard work of getting ready for the cold weather is
finally over, and we can relax 'til the snow gets deep.*

November

A time of year to show that we are truly thankful.
This is a time of loving, sharing, and showing others
we are caring.
It is the time we show our duty to our government.
Voting for the right person to represent us is
our command.
Veterans are honored for protecting their land.
We are showing the world as a
people, united we stand.
We are proud community of many
a race, color, and creed.
A time for thanking those who
went on before, defending
a land others have freed.
This is a time of Thanksgiving, and the love of God
in whom we put our trust.
A prayer to God, I say is a must.
November is a month of loving humanity.

Author's Comment:
*Remember from where we come, and the reason
for this coming season!*

Thanks Giving Special

Just listening to those old turkey hunters??
Papa said, "There's nothing better than wild turkey
fer Thanks Givin' dinner.
This bought bird jest didn't have
the flavor within her.
We ought to go huntin' fer one of them ole birds."
Mama said, "Well, I think that's quite absurd."
Well Papa kept tellin' her not to buy one.
We'd be goin' out there to get the job done.
With guns in hand here all three of us stand.
Excitement mountin' as we head
for the wooded land.
Like hunters of long ago off to get
that ole turkey we did go.
We walked for what seemed to be hours, findin'
nothin' don't ya know.
We all sat down to take a short rest.
Papa dropped his gun, and it went off!
Nervous and confused I fell to the ground.
As I lay there I heard an awful crashin' sound?
From a nearby tree a raccoon came runnin' down.
The raccoon, scared by the loud bang, ran away.

Papa, a little bewildered, didn't
know just what to say.
Well, when we got ourselves together, we
decided we didn't want turkey anyway?
Mama, expectin' a miracle, was cookin' the rest
of our dinner.
Dressin,' squash, green beens, and taters.
"Nothin' there to make Uncle Joe any thinner."
She baked a choice of punkin' or apple pie.
"It smells so good," we said with a sigh.
Well, when we told her, "No turkey," we
wanted to die.
This year we had ham sandwiches with all the fixins.

December

Winter is here, and the cold weather
has set in.
Skiing, skating, and snow sports to win.
Come on in—sit down—we have a football
team to cheer.
Hurry all around to get the presents for
loved ones so dear.
This is the time for giving, sharing, loving,
and caring.
December is the very last month of the year.
This kind of life is truly great, right to the end.
Helping others to have a good Christmas
with family and friends.
With loving kindness like this there
is nothing to fear.
This I say to you my friend.
Have a Happy New Year.

On A Winter's Night

To all who love life in all its forms!

Snow-covered land with dark, shadowed trees
are a wonderful sight.
The cold and quiet winter's night is shown
with the full moon bright.
Some deer out playing and kicking up the snow.
While others arc calmly eating those stubborn
apples that did not fall.
Just see the wildlife here in the country
where livin' is a ball.
It is a sight to behold—the beauty
that God has given all.
The wonders of seeing the dove resting in the trees.
The wild turkey marching single file as
pretty as you please.
The beauty of God's creation just for us to see.
God has surely blessed us this
winter Christmas Eve!

Author's Comment:
Merry Christmas to everyone!

The Reason For Christmas

Christmas is not just for the coming season, it's
for eternity!!!

The love for mankind and the beauty that
God has made.
The truth of creation at my feet is laid.
If you simply put the puzzle together in the way
it is meant to be,
you'd find the only message sent from above.
Why God sent His Son for all the world to see.
Showing us His greatness and the meaning of
true love.
The love of mankind and the beauty that God
has made.
The truth of creation at my feet is laid.
The sun above and the earth below.
Peace in my heart as on through life I go.
Baby Jesus is only part of the wonderful story.
Jesus as a boy, prophet, and teacher.
Telling of His Father above and how He made
each earthly creature.
Teaching of the good and bad, and eternal
love.
Showing us a picture of our Father above.

Looking to the sun above and the earth below.
Peace in my heart as on through life I go.

Author's Comment:
Why do I live? Because of God's grace!

My Christmas Gift

To all who will listen!!

As I look around at others I see
a little of you and a little of me.
We all are very much the same, don't you see?
The young are looking for fun, and being carefree,
just as we used to be.
There are some that are
looking to things of gain—riches.
Others look to knowledge for
fixing life's little glitches.
The truth is that all this is nothing but a distraction.
The love of God should be our center of attraction.
So my Christmas gift to you this year will be
a prayer to God that you will see the mercies
and guidance He gives to you and me.

Author's Comment:
*I feel that a prayer for each other would be the best
Gift we could possibly give.*

My Military Career

USS Yorktown (CVS 10)

Displacement: 27,100 tons
Length: 872 feet
Beam: 93 feet—extreme width
at flight deck: 147 feet
Draft: 28 feet 7 inches
Speed: 32.7 knots
Complement: 3,448 crew
Armament: 12 five-inch guns, 32
(40mm.) guns, 46 (20mm.) guns
Aircraft: 80+
Class: Essex

This was the fourth ship named the *Yorktown*, and she was laid down on 1 December 1941. She was built by the Newport News Shipbuilding & Drydock Co. as the *Homme Richard*, renamed *USS Yorktown* on 26 September 1942. The *USS Yorktown* was launched on 21 January 1943, sponsored by Mrs. Eleanor Roosevelt, and commissioned on 15 April 1943 at the Norfolk, VA, Navy Yard with Captain Joseph J. "Jocko" Clark in command. The *Yorktown* remained in the Norfolk area until 21 May 1943. She got underway to the Trinidad

area for her shakedown training. She returned to
Norfolk on 17 June and began her post shake-
down availability. The aircraft carrier completed
repairs needed on 1 July and began air operations
out of Norfolk until 6 July. She then exited the
Chesapeake Bay on her way to the Pacific Ocean.
I joined up with her in Japan for my tour
of sea duty. She had already started the
six month West-Pac deployment from her
home port of Long Beach, California.

The Fighting Lady
(1962–1965)

*It was a special occasion in my life, and
I am proud to have served on her.*

As a young sailor I thought there
was none that could beat her.
She was my first; I flew to Japan to meet her.
They were just hoisting the anchor
when I got to greet her.
We were leaving the Japanese shore
and headed for Viet Nam.
Showing her great power, sending a message for the
communists to scram.
The *Yorktown,* one of the best in our fleet.
She finished her work and headed back
to Long Beach, pier "E" street.
Oh, but the weather was getting seriously bad.
The Admiral called short the liberty we just had.
The order was to cut the lines and head for sea.
A great storm of all things it had to be.
The ocean got rough, and the
waves started crashing high.
I was in wonder as the wind gave a ghostly cry.
Up into the Alaskan straits our lady did go.
It looked as if the ship left the water below.

The waves rose to forty or fifty feet high.
It was as if they were trying to reach the sky.
A storm like this being so mean is
something I'd never seen.
The lady fought that storm with all of her might.
The seas finally calmed; we pulled
into port that following night.
The *Yorktown* sailors went on
liberty. They had earned that right.

Author's Comment:
*I loved that old ship, and if you want to see her, she's
docked at Charleston, SC, as a museum.*

USS Gray
(FF-1054)

To our NAVY, and sea power!

A Navy ship of tremendous power.
High above the San Diego pier did she tower.
She was a beautiful lady all the
sailors learned to love.
Her mission that year to sail a world tour spreading
peace as America's dove,
for the sailors aboard her was a special treat.
We were going to Indonesia, Fiji, Taiwan, Tasmania,
New Zealand, Australia, and the
Philippines—for their people to meet.
The lady left America's shores
in September of 1977.
You'd almost think those
sailors were going straight to heaven.
We visited those wonderful
countries with diplomatic tact.
This I can honestly say that
serving in the Navy was no act.
It was very real, that cruise called West-Pac.

Author's Comment:
This was the cruise of 6 September '77 to April '78.

USS Tecumseh
(SSBN-628)

To the boat's namesake, the man: Tecumseh.

In a Navy of strength and power.
Tecumseh came to help in a needed hour.
In a time when the cold war was very strong.
He showed his color loud and long.
He spent his time in the silent and deep.
With the bravest of men our way of life to keep.
Like namesake, Tecumseh is strong and true.
Protection for a way of life and freedom too.
What about the man for which
this submarine was named?
A great American before America it became.
Born around 1768 this man loved
his people and his land.
As a young man he rose up to the battle's demand.
Walking tall among his broth-
ers, talking peace to abide.
"Keep the Indian nations together
with strength and pride."
Tecumseh knew that the white man would win
no matter what he tried.

For his people and for his land he died.
Strength and power for world peace was his desire.
A true American even before it came to be.
Tecumseh was strong, straight,
and tall as all could see.
A man of peace in times of aggression,
he held his head high through a proud
people's depression.
I am honored to have served
under such a great name.

Author's Comment:
*It was truly a great honor to serve with some of the
Navy's best sailors.*

VP-50 In Viet Nam

The Navy's eye in the sky.

That is where the squadron's duties lie.
To watch the waters of this embattled war zone.
Pride and honor as we worked long hours each day.
The aircraft (*P-3C Orion*) is a
solid foundation to lay.
Watching the coast, keeping dangerous ships and
cargo out of our way.
The power of modern
electronics clearly guarding the coast.
True naval power that America can boast.
Our Naval Air Squadrons are a great way to say,
"We will keep the enemies of our country at bay."

Author's Comment:
*I served with both VP-50 and VP-49 while living
a great twenty-year career in the Navy.*

A Soldier

To the honor of a Soldier on Veteran's Day.

I am a soldier of this great land.
I have gone to war to make a freedom stand.
Ready to protect America from oppression at
the first command.
Feelings of love and duty to protect my fellow man.
To guard the hopes and dreams
of people just like you.
People like Mom, Dad, Uncle
Frank, and Aunt Wilma too.
The reason I go is so close to me,
and the list a mile long.
The thoughts and memories have long since
been written in song.
Friends and loved ones I've counted by the score.
Think of all those brave men and women
that have gone on before.
Also the working man, his family, and his wife.
The chance for a time of peace without fear of strife.
Mostly I do this work of danger for what I believe.
This powerful nation and words of it that I perceive.
My belief in a great and powerful God.

The love I have for where I live on this
American sod.
It is not the revenge or hate—or to even the score.
It is for truth, love, and the grace of God galore.
This is why I decided to go to war.

Author's Comment:
*It takes a very big man or woman to face the picture
of death so others can enjoy freedom!*

Freedom

Freedom is a word each of us in dif-
ferent ways define.
Most cherish the thoughts to be sublime.
Others feel it to be doing just for
themself and not for you.
Freedom for all is quite the dream and not the rule.
If you think you are the only one
around, you're the fool.
Freedom is like love—you have to give to keep it.
You can't demand, command, or try to take it.
You can't fake it, but you can forsake it.
Freedom is a fragile thing.
Freedom for all is quite the dream and not the rule.
If you think you are the only one
around, you're the fool.
Please understand—the
freedom that you can command
is your love for a fellow man.
Freedom is love that you give, not
the hate that you take.
Show the world how to love before it is too late.

Look around at all the hate, and
you can foresee our fate.
Freedom for all is quite the dream and not the rule.
If you think you are the only one
around, you're the fool.

Looking Past The Moment

To all Americans who care!

Revenge and hate is not in my heart.
Looking to the end as we did the start.
Down down the towers, but raise up the spirit.
Down down the towers, all power to our land.
This land under God let it be!
Sorrow and sadness will always
be a part of you and me.
Thousands gone from life into
memory, but God still guides
Us, don't you see?
Down down the towers, but raise up the spirit.
Down down the towers, all power to our land.
People helping people—they are
all just like you and me.
War against the crime, not at the man.
Let the courts of justice stand.
Sorrow and sadness will always
be a part of you and me.
Thousands gone from life into
memory, but God still guides
Us, don't you see?
Down down the towers, but raise up the spirit.

Down down the towers, all power to our land.
This nation under God let it be!

Author's Comment:
This poem I wrote on September 19, 2001, just after the terrible attack by terrorists on New York City. I tried to show the grief, sadness, and anger of that inhumane act.

The Battle

*To all True Christians that are fight-
ing the good fight for souls.*

In the battle of life we only stand one chance.
Study your Bible to know the truth in advance.
Keep a sharp eye for the devil's tricks,
or on your grave he will dance.
Shame, fear, and doubts are on
the attacks from the side.
Watch your back, because he is sending a
barrage of pride.
Hate, spite, and revenge will
advance in the dark of night.
Be strong and brave staying down
in your bunker of faith.
Remember: reinforcements from heaven are
behind us all the way.
Protecting and guiding you every step of the way.
So fight the good fight, and save a mother, brother,
sister, or friend.
Know in your heart the strongest weapon around
is the prayer you send.

Author's Comment:
My prayers are with all of you!

My Faith

God Forgives, And So Can I

*All the things wrong with life around us,
we need forgiveness!*

You and I are sinners, we have to agree.
When we are wrong, don't just let it be.
Ask God to forgive and set you free.
Know in your heart God is there for you
and me.
God is watching and waiting for us in His
home in the sky.
From me to you, "God forgives," and so can I.
If you see your brother stumble, take his hand.
If you hear yours sister's sorrow, strike up
the band.
If your brother and sister go wrong, pray they
take their stands.
Praise the living God for making this our
precious land.
Know in your heart that God is with you
even after you die.
From me to you, "God forgives," and so can I.

Destiny

Yes, we have choices in our lives, and nothing
else do we bring.
We were all put here to do one certain thing.
The choices we make put into
play all the things we do.
It could be something easy like
just being friends with you.
It could be something hard, real
hard—like the universe to know.
It could be the weather man
telling how the wind will blow.
How about leading your
country for just a little while.
A designer coming up with a new
fad or that latest style.
It really doesn't matter of all the things you may be.
When it's over God is who we will see.
The last moment of judgment is for you and me.
That, my friend, is our true destiny.

Author's Comment:
There is a beginning and an end. We don't bring
anything in, and we can't take anything out. It is where
we are going that counts!

God

To stress, and how it can tear up our lives if we let it!!

When the storms of life are too big to bare.
When the world around you seems not to care.
When you stand alone, but don't really dare.
When all the dark clouds block you from your goal.
Just remember, my friend, that God is in control!

Incarnate

To those that are Christians, but afraid of the world!

As God is with us, and we with He.
The mirror-shown tools of the
Carpenter let you see.
Missions around the world no matter where.
He is there with me.
The devil working in his extreme ways.
Be careful of the problems, barriers, he will raise.
Tell God while in prayer, and that will put a stop
to the tricks he plays.
Keep in mind, "With God you
win, and the devil you lose."
Let God do his work through you
and spread the good news.
God never said being a Christian would be easy.
So come out to the mission field and pay your dues.
Spend your time on this old earth let-
ting others know:
the love of God is the only way to go!

Author's Comment:
So many Christians today go to Church, and that's it.
They very seldom take Christ to work with them. Is
He a part of your life, or is He your whole life?

Look Into The Heart Of God

To all who look for the beauty in life!

Look to the mountains. See their strong beauty.
Look deep within your heart for love and duty.
Look to the green meadows and the cold, flowing
water of a stream.
Look into your heart for that
sweet and gentle dream.
Look to the mist of the calm, sooth-
ing rain from above.
Look into the eyes of family and
friends—the ones you love.
Look at the wonders of a sun-
set at the end of a truly great day.
Look into the blessed "Living Word"
and the things it will say.
Look at the flowers of spring com-
ing up from the sod.
All of this is where you can see
into the heart of God!

Do The Dead Speak?

Have you had a loved one die then at
a later date heard that voice?

I believe this truth is from the grace of God.
Sometimes He uses friends and
relatives to guide us along.
They come to us through our thoughts
and actions, where they belong.
They keep us out of trouble and from all wrong.
Do you doubt that what I'm
singing is really in the song?
Look in the Bible to Genesis, it tells of
Abel crying out from the ground.
That, my friend, is not all for after
thousands of years gone down.
Abel in Hebrews is back, and his
speaking does abound.
This, dear friend, with God's
loving care He wants us to see.
To follow the Ten Commandments it has to be!

Author's Comment:
When making decisions I sometimes turn to hear my
mother say, 'Be patient, and think things out before
going ahead,' or other things she used to say when she
was living.

Make The Change

To the one looking for the real truth!

The Day of Judgment is upon us.
Know that what you do is in his trust.
What you say to me in reality means little.
At times the words said are in a lying riddle.
What you speak is what you live.
Don't let it be, ask, and God will forgive.
Listen to Jesus, and you'll start a trend.
Show God's love by telling your friend.
Color and race will no longer have a place.
We are brothers and sisters all because of Jesus
and God's loving grace.
Sin will be driven from your heart.
The fullness of God's love gives us a new start.
A verse from the Psalm should be a must.
"Preserve me, O God, for in thee do I put my trust."

Author's Comment:
*You will find the real truth only in the living word of
God!*

How Long Is Your Life

To those who want to know.

Do you know when you'll die?
Life could be gone in a wink of an eye.
If we only knew we could be ready.
Our lives would be more sure and steady.
You may get to thinking you're real cool.
If you believe that you are a fool.
So if you are smart you'll not wait.
Take time to look back on what you have done.
It's not too late to change the ways of your life.
Living the bondage of hatred and strife.
What you have done with your life God will know.
Understand at time of judg-
ment there is no place to go.
Where are you heading as time flies by?
Knowing and believing in your
Savior before you die,
that is something you should try.

Four Rode Horses

I had a dream last night; just hope that is what it
is to be.
A prayer for wisdom so everyone's eye can see.
My dream tells of what could hap-
pen to you and me.
The first of the four riders on a white horse just
appeared on our land.
A bow and a crown for the conqueror to
command.
This leader masquerades the truth to hold control,
but only a short stand.
The second rider comes on a red horse.
His intentions are of blood and
destruction, of course.
Murder and war after war is what he does, and
that comes from a mighty good source.
In time a third rider comes racing in on a black
horse to take the scene.
Famine and hard times are what it will mean.
He lives to see people in pain as life's
necessities are few and far between.

I fear to look at this rider of a
pale horse here within.
He is the cause of sorrow and death from all
worldly sin.
I watched all this take place from Heaven's door.
As I heard a sad and lonely sound of a lost
world of sin straight to the core.
Well, then I awoke to see it wasn't done, but
there was more.
I am truly glad for the warning of the
Revelation!
It's because of *Christ* and the face of
Salvation!

No Fear In Faith

There is no fear in faith.
King David knew very well.
He was a strong believer in Heaven and Hell.
The courage God gave to him as a small boy,
he used for a giant to destroy.
When his enemies tried to down him,
just one word from God, and they fell.
Psalm 23 tells God is there with us
so fear not at all.
Then Psalm 118:6 says, "The Lord is on my side;
I will not fear.
What can man do unto me?"
When God speaks the devil will flee!

The Towers We Build

You can have your mansion here;
I want mine in Heaven.

It seems we all want to be seen and heard.
Thinking we're better than others is absurd.
The problem is not doing our very best.
Challenge is just putting our body to the test.
Running the race with a
winning spirit is simply great.
The sporting way would be a wonderful fate.
When we put into our mind that
we are too good to associate.
We feel others don't measure up,
causing us to segregate.
As time goes by that thought
most always turns to hate.
Groups of people that could have been friends
now at war right up to the very end.
God forgive us, and help to change this trend!

Author's Comment:
Where is your heart?

Christ Is Born

As we look back at the
special splendor of our Savior!

Shorter the days and longer the nights.
Winter is here in our sights.
Cold winds blow big drifts of snow.
Think of the first Christmas long, long ago—
happy season of home fires burning bright.
If you go out, bundle up real tight.
Children sledding up on the hill.
Joy in your hearts with thoughts of goodwill.
Come out to the barn, and feed
the animals some corn.
Blessed Christmas for it's our Savior that is born!

Author's Comment:
This is my version of a seasonal view at Christmas.

I Heard No One Pray

To all good Christian Americans
who care for our country!

Look at the sin and corruption in our streets.
Through all this violence the population, we deplete.
Talking down our friends and neigh-
bors we think is real neat.
Trust and caring seem almost gone, you say.
Well, this I will say: "I heard no one pray."
A friend needs help, but you walk the other way.
Listen to the people and just hear
what they have to say
as they turn to the darkness when
the law they should obey.
Well, this I will say: "I heard no one pray!"
What will you do if God comes here today?

Author's Comment:
When you really look at the truth you know we have but
a little time here on earth!

The Coat Of Many Colors

For people trying to live a lie.

We each wear a coat for all to see.
Look at your life, and where Christ should be.
The blood-stained garment is the
sin that he paid for me.
As a Christian, do we tell of it true?
Do we tell it as it is, or make a fable new?
No matter what you show the world,
God will show the truth as it is unfurled.
So as the lies of the little coat of old,
your life by how it is lived is how your soul is sold.
I ask you now to look deep into your heart.
Pray to God for help and a wonderful new start!

Judge Not

*We all make the mistake of trying to judge
others (look in the mirror).*

Look unto others as less than I.
This we do and know not why.
Gossip or lying considered a curse.
Be a killer or a thief, what may be worse?
Try hate or even pride, but don't get involved.
Sin is sin, and the worst can not be solved.
As humans we live, and humans we are.
Drink at home or at a bar.
Those others, "Oh, they are wrong!"
Look in the mirror before you sing that song.
Well, who is the judge, surely not you?
Only our maker can say what is so.
Until that time only one thing you should know.
Have love in your heart and let
all other thoughts go.
Look into your own heart to see God's answer grow.

Power

You tell me!

What do you see that is true power?
Maybe it is time itself, keep all within the hour?
Could it be that power is like a mighty waterfall?
How about the giant Redwood trees so very tall?
Would it be as the Alps, mountains that seem to
touch the sky?
Maybe the universe beyond the imagination it's
so high?
Try on true love and the power it can do.
In my mind it is the Creator of me and you!
What about a fierce tiger? Oh, but he's just a
little kitty.
Maybe you see power as the great skyscraper
of a big city?
Could be the genius ability of the computer
construction?
How about a tornado or hurricane with winds
of destruction?
Would you say it was the power
of the super information
highways?

Your country's government, you might say?
Try on true love and the power it can do.
In my mind it's the Creator of me and you!!

Author's Comment:
There's a lot of talk about power, but I feel there is none greater than God!

What Do We Know

Time, patience, and God will give you the good life!

Each day is never like the day before.
New feelings, hopes, and dreams galore.
At times it will seem very hard, and at
others just a complete bore.
At last the time of what to do in life
is yours to decide.
As years go by everything seems magnified.
If when young you listen and learn,
chances are very good.
You are where your ancestors stood.
As time goes by and you start to look back.
You will see things to what you lack.
Better feelings, hopes, and dreams
for the child in what you see.
Nothing you can do, but hope and
pray you gave that child
a good start.
Leave it all to the young for now it is time for
you to depart.
If the truth of life you've learned.
The road to Heaven you have earned.

Author's Comment:

*Our whole life we look for what we think is the rightway
in hopes we did it right.*

The Greatest Gift God Gave To Me

God gave me my eyes to see the beauty of
nature so grand.
He gave me my mouth to speak the truth,
and not a lie on the other hand.
God gave me feet to stand upon, and be
counted with my fellow man.
He gave me my hands to greet, and
help the whole human clan.
He gave me my head to think of the
wonders of His great plan.
Most of all God gave me a heart so
from within I could see.
His tremendous tender love for me!

Author's Comment:
God's love is why He gave us salvation by His grace.

Just Thinking (Only My Opinion)

Love

To all who are looking for love!!

I feel we've forgotten what love really means.
Listen and watch the TV screen.
Selling sex is what they do, but their meaning
of love is not true.
God has shown the love that's right for me
and you.
Love is caring, helping, and sharing—the kind we
ought to learn.
If you are looking for true love, that you
will have to earn!

Beauty Is Only Skin Deep

How is your mirror Image???

Take a look into all of nature and you will see:
the prettiest flower is generally poison as it can be.
Look at the blue jay, he's as vain as
anything, don't you agree?
I think if he were in music class, he'd get a D!
Try that sleek, shiny black crow, he
steals all he can get, don't you know.
Off to his nest with treasure he will go.
Oh, you might take a distant glance
at the pretty little skunk.
Got too close and you found
how bad he really stunk.
This with people so often has
the same age-old trends.
The just plain Jim and Jane aren't
good enough to be friends.
Handsome or pretty; when you look
in the mirror, what do you see?
Is it someone you think is better than him, or me?
Well, just think about the blue jay, crow, and skunk.
You may have had the personality that really stunk!

Author's Comment:
The most precious beauty is in the heart!

Looking For The Leader

Mama is busy in the kitchen, and
Dad is working in the field.
Mama fixin' a good and healthy
meal the family to feed.
Dad, well, he's plantin' the crops in the
ground, looking for a great yield.
Mama? She's teachin' all us kids our
school lessons and how to read.
Dad is getting the cows in the barn, so
he can have the milking done.
Mama is in a hurry loading dirty clothes
in the washer, a job that's no
fun.
This is a typical day here in the
country of our family on the run.
The day is finally over, and we all sit down to dinner.
Heads bowed, and hands clasped, we
ask God to bless this farm family.
With *God* as our leader, this family is the winner!

Junk Mail

Catalogs, ads, and lotteries you can send in.
The garbage mail you get has got to be a sin.
Junk mail is part of the world we have made.
I guess we just put up with this junk mail parade.
Enticements for you to get a credit card.
You have to really watch out and be on your guard.
Ads that tell you, "Spend, spend,
spend—that will be okay."
Oh, who needs money anyway?
The junk mail you get has to be a sin.
What can you do? You surely can't win!
Catalogues and ads that say you
have to spend to save.
Listen to them and your credit will cave.
The idea is, don't listen to just anyone!
Think things out and get your bills on the run.
You'll be debt free and live happily under the sun.

Author's Comment:
Take a good look around. Americans are in debt, and
in trouble!

Time Flies

All of us older folks.

A fast-paced life seems to be the way.
Curse of curses, I would say.
Just a few hours from dusk 'til dawn.
As I blink the years have come and gone.
All the joys and sadnesses are only memories.
The end of life comes all too fast.
After all, we knew it couldn't last.
Advice to you, my friend, take note of your behavior.
Use more of your time to talk to
God, your heavenly savior.

Author's Comment:
*Life is too short, and we don't know when it will end.
We better be ready for that time.*

The Old Lighthouse

*People work hard and care until
they are old. Then what?*

Look at the old lighthouse up on that rocky ledge.
For many, many years it has given
sailors a certain edge.
It stands there so brave and all alone.
Telling the ships that this is their danger zone.
Helping to guide them all safely in.
No matter how bad the stormy wind.
Look up at that old lighthouse now.
Left on that rocky ledge alone, because
we no longer need it now.

Author's Comment:
This is the fate of many of our older citizens!

Just Getting Along

To people that just exist.

Everyday is just what you make it.
If you let everyone else tell you
how, they will break it.
Take charge; even if you don't know how, fake it.
After all the day is yours, so don't
let someone else take it.
Stand up and let them know who is in charge.
Try being more like that old tug
boat and not like the barge.
What would it look like if the recruit was shouting
orders at the Sarge?
Look at life in a new perspective.
A prayer to God so he'll be protective.
That, my friend, is what life is all about.
So now, go on, and let it all hang out!

Take Time

If there isn't enough time in your day!

In today's fast-paced life, there is no time to waste.
You hurry to work to protect your
career and do your best.
Your wife rushes around to clean the house, so when
you get there the dinner you can taste.
Are you just too busy to stop and rest?
Working so hard to pay all those bills.
Barely enough each week if there are no frills.
Just not the time to get everything done.
Goodness gracious, don't you have any fun?
Sit down for a few minutes; plan your things out.
Take the time to find what life is all about.
No need to run, because living isn't a race.
Use your time to work and sleep, but don't forget
that fun has its place.
Love your life because you've got-
ten it through God's grace.

Author's Comment:
Life is a gift use it well!

True Friends

To all who love God!!

The beauty of friendship is know-
ing you are not alone.
Sharing our mistakes, we need others to atone—
ones we give trust, our problems to be dissolved.
Never do true friends come to a place of resolve.
At time we feel no one cares.
Thoughts like that we should resist.
Our friends won't let those feelings persist.
My true friend sends His love from above.
He let Noah know by sending him a dove.
All you have to do to have a friend like mine.
On bended knees talk to Him in prayer.
Ask forgiveness while there is still time left to share!

Author's Comment:
*I truly believe that if you give Him a chance your heart
will allow honest love in.*

Credit Cards

*To all the people that have debt problems because
of credit cards.*

It's good if only used in emergencies as cash.
It's great to get your gas and pay
at the pump in a flash.
No carrying all that money around in your pocket.
Slap that card down for a gift,
a necklace, or a locket.
Oops, there we are on the go again!
You better slow down and think it over, my friend.
I guess you could call it a temptation card?
Just spend and spend, that is all. Too easy.
It's all the damage you've done; that makes it hard.
Looking at the monthly
statement will make you *queasy!*
The credit card with a little
common sense is real good.
To use it for what it's meant for
has to be understood.
Keep a close eye on what you have to spend.
You'll have it in control, less trouble in the end!

Author's Comment:
Credit cards are the most dangeous things ever invented.

Money

Don't make money an idol!! It won't pay.

Money is minerals of the land.
Money is power in the hand.
No money causes great stress.
Money through working is truly blessed.
Money gotten by crime? You're gonna do time.
Money all spent will make you sad.
Money can be very good or very bad.
Trusting in money will make you too late.
Putting money over God, and
there will be no pearly gate.

Author's Comment:
Money can be the root of all evil!

Talk To The Dead

The sight at the death of a loved one.

Going north to get to east.
Sitting here waiting for the beast.
If only the truth be known,
society I'll drop on my own.
Dark side to hide from my sight.
Act the part of its very height.
Save the day and hold back the night.
I look at you with a heart of sadness.
When I come, it will be with a
soul filled with gladness.

Author's Comment:
*With a tortured soul we watch our friends go on before us,
but at the end we'll meet again.*

Thunder In The Dark

Just a thought?

Take it all in: the smell, the sight, and sound.
This country's beauty is lying all around.
The smell of the wind blowing in the trees.
The sight of a horse in the meadow, mane and tail
flowing in the breeze.
Listen to the meadowlark or the
crash of thunder in the dark.
Yes, country beauty is everywhere to be found.
Take time to know the
treasures of this earth's ground.
The sight of the moon and stars in the sky.
The true treasures are ones you just can't buy.
Can you feel the jumping in your
heart as lightning makes
it's first spark?
Then listen to the roar of thunder in the dark.
Life is full of joy and fears from the very first start.
Don't worry about the small things,
because they will soon depart.
Time cares for all nature's work, so
don't upset the apple cart.
Listen and you will hear the thunder in the dark.

The American Indian

To my brother, the true American.

Man came in ships of wood to
take this land from me.
This land of plenty we knew, so helping them
was the good thing to do.
Enough land for both me and you.
Soon they took from me just for their own greed.
Planting the blood of sorrow in
my people was their seed.
Promising all, and giving none, was their honor
and their call.
Making prisoners and slaves of us all.
The time has come when even our memories try
to leave our soul.
You see the truth of me, so for
whom does your bell toll?
Not the Indian who trusted you, but the ones
that call themselves Americans.

Author's Comment:
*I am not an Indian, but by reading our History, I feel I
understand the pain.*

Listen

The Bible tells us, "If you have an ear, listen!"

Canadian, American, Chinese, and
Indian all are people like you.
Russian, English, Spanish, and French,
are truly good people too.
From Adam we all did come.
Greed and pride to fuel our fears.
Fighting and killing throughout the years.
Baptist, Catholic, Methodist, too—all
with somewhat misguided view.
Man has always seen only his
own personal thoughts.
The very reason so many battles have been fought.
It is time for all humanity to see eye to
eye and praise our God on high.
All the books of religion teach of love.
Stop the madness and listen to
the message from above!

The Sparrow

I always think it is a joy to watch the birds
in the winter.
The sparrow is such a common little bird.
The whole idea of flying south is quite absurd.
A tough, little guy staying in the north all year long.
He is always happy singing his beautiful song.
The way he flies around so fast,
I think it's kind of neat.
He loves the tall grasses of the meadow,
a place to put his feet.
A seed here, and a seed there,
makes his dinner complete.
In winter he comes over to see if
I've filled his plate with food.
It would be a sad place here
without this wonderful little dude!

Coupons

To all who are just trying to make ends meet.

Living good on a budget is no dream.
It saves some of your money for the cream.
Watch the ads sent from the store.
Check the newspaper, and you
might save even more.
Use only the coupons for things on your list.
It helps the extra spending to resist.
Give excess coupons you do not
use to a friend in need.
Sharing with others is a wonderful creed.
To the coupons, and your budget, a good luck
I do send.
Making your money fit your
budget is a rule to defend!

Decisions

To all that aren't afraid to face the truth!

Looking around at all there is to see,
there's nothing hard in life for me.
We all have choices in what we do.
That is what truly makes us free.
Do the good or bad, the right or wrong,
and face the consequences that will be.
The one who is in doubt really has no life at all.
Doing the right or wrong in another person's mind
has to be your call.
If you do what works for you, your life will be a ball.
A little love, a little care, and a lot of prayer.
This makes life something others want to share!

Just Love Remembering

To all us old folks?

Looking back to when times were hard.
Grandma's doughnuts fried in a hot pan of lard.
Us kids playin' kick the can out in the yard.
Get workin' out in the fields all day.
Feedin' the cows and bringin' in the hay.
All us kids gone down to the creek to play.
Sit down to supper, holdin' each
other's hands as we prayed.
Thank God for His guidance and
that the bills were paid.
Pet the dog as by my chair he laid.
Sit on the porch just watchin' the sun go down.
Get to bed early cause
tomorrow the county fair is in town.
I guess I couldn't say life was all that hard.
Think back; when all this
happened, we had the penny postcard.

Author's Comment:
Can you tell how long ago this was?

Why?

To all who wonder why did God do all of this for us.

Why did God create you and me?
Why did He make the universe for us to see?
Why does man doubt all the
wonder that came to be?
The great detail and beauty He put into a tree.
Why did God make my heart so
it could be easily broken?
The truth and love that He gave
us wasn't just a token.
The eyes he gave me to see the wonder and beauty.
Why did God give man a brain to make a choice?
Why did He let man his thoughts to voice?
Why does man try his best to destroy it all?
Why did God let man make that call?
It is all because of the love He has for me.
Oh, what an extraordinary God He happens to be!
I am looking forward to being
with Him for all eternity!

Help Humanity

We have a very beautiful land, so why do we try
our best to destroy it?

Cry, coyote, cry—and let the eagle fly.
Try your best to make us understand.
Leading us back to this, our beautiful land.
Teach us not to poison our environment,
or there'll be nothing for our retirement.
Cry, coyote, cry—and let the eagle fly.
Make your plea loud and clear, so men
of science can hear.
Make the message loud and strong.
Sound the warning from all the mountains
with a song.
Cry, coyote, cry—and let the eagle fly.
Cheer us on to help with this great task.
From nature we have lots of forgiveness to ask.
If only nature and humanity could get along,
what pleasure God would see.
This job will take us all, including you and me!

Nation Of Pets

For all you who care.

Dogs and cats are our friends, we say.
We love to watch them as they play.
They are honest and true, extremely faithful, too.
We don't give them credit where credit is due.
We just let them run when they are no more fun.
We even forget them before the day is done.
They leave because they can't tell us we're wrong.
They know when our loyalty is gone.
Across the lawn, and out in the street,
cars they are trying to beat.
They aren't fast enough to reach the other side.
Poor lonely pet laying in the street where it died.

Author's Comment:
*So many times we see this happen, and it does not have to
be. It's a shame that we have to bear it.*

I

I is such a selfish word.
Most likely it starts every war that ever occurred.
I seems to make each of us feel very strong.
Putting *I* all alone makes for a sad, sad song.
We soon learn that *I* can't do it all.
Say a little prayer, and God will answer the call.
Learn to be happy by knowing that you and me
add up to *we*.
This way you will never be alone, don't you see?
Love your neighbor as yourself.
Go ahead. Put their picture up on your shelf.
You will find that love keeps
growing right to the end.
Loving our Heavenly Father will give back
the greatest dividends.

Author's Comment:
The human heart can't stand loneliness!

How Old Is Old

Relax, it's time to sit back and enjoy life.

"How old is old?" you say.
Looking back you can see old in many a way.
Old can be one child looking up to another,
even how some children look at their mothers.
A teen just graduated from school.
It could be that old means you and me.
Just look around at old, but be gentle and kind.
Because old is only in your own mind.
Use your time wisely with thoughts of where you
are going, and where you've been.
The truth of the matter is how
you treat your friends.

Retired

To all us old wrinkled folks out there.

I think it's great to be old.
Sitting here under the old apple tree.
It's nice to know how great life can be.
Just relax, and watch the world go by,
feeling the warm summer sun
come down from the sky.
Through good times and bad, it's
friends that keep me goin.
The summer sun is gone, and the
north wind starts to blowin.'
Life has been so good, I think I'll sing a tune.
Nothing to worry about it will be over soon.
It's time you retire and sit with me
under this old apple tree.

Author's Comment:
Enjoy what you've got!

Just so my sister gets in the book.